טוב

MARTIAL ARTS
KUNG FU

by Tim O'Shei

Reading Consultant:
Barbara J. Fox
Reading Specialist
North Carolina State University

Content Consultant:
Sifu Brad Ryan, 10th Generation Disciple
Mengs Martial Arts/Hung Fa Kwoon
Houston, Texas

Mankato, Minnesota

Blazers is published by Capstone Press,
151 Good Counsel Drive, P.O. Box 669, Mankato, Minnesota 56002.
www.capstonepress.com

Copyright © 2009 by Capstone Press, a Capstone Publishers company. All rights reserved.
No part of this publication may be reproduced in whole or in part, or stored in a retrieval
system, or transmitted in any form or by any means, electronic, mechanical,
photocopying, recording, or otherwise, without written permission of the publisher.
For information regarding permission, write to Capstone Press,
151 Good Counsel Drive, P.O. Box 669, Dept. R, Mankato, Minnesota 56002.
Printed in the United States of America

Library of Congress Cataloging-in-Publication Data
O'Shei, Tim.
    Kung fu / by Tim O'Shei.
    p. cm. — (Blazers. Martial arts)
    Includes bibliographical references and index.
    Summary: "Discusses the history, techniques, ranks, and competitions of
kung fu" — Provided by publisher.
    ISBN-13: 978-1-4296-1963-9 (hardcover)
    ISBN-10: 1-4296-1963-5 (hardcover)
    1. Kung fu — Juvenile literature. I. Title.
GV1114.7.O84 2009
796.815'9 — dc22   2007052210

Essential content terms are **bold** and are defined on the spread where they first appear.

Editorial Credits
Abby Czeskleba, editor; Ted Williams, designer; Jo Miller, photo researcher;
    Sarah L. Schuette, photo shoot direction; Marcy Morin, scheduler

Photo Credits
All principle photography by Capstone Press/Karon Dubke except:
Getty Images Inc./Cancan Chu, 7; National Geographic/Justin
    Guariglia, 5, 9
Landov LLC/Xinhua, 25
Zuma Press/Courtesy of Revolution/Columbia Studios/F. Masi, 27; Lonely
    Planet Images/Greg Elms, 19

The Capstone Press Photo Studio thanks the members of the Mankato Kung Fu
Association in Mankato, Minnesota, for their assistance with photo shoots for
this book.

1 2 3 4 5 6 13 12 11 10 09 08

TABLE OF CONTENTS

CHAPTER 1:
The Shaolin Temple................. 4

CHAPTER 2:
Practicing Kung Fu................. 10

CHAPTER 3:
Colors and Ranks.................. 18

CHAPTER 4:
Kung Fu Competitions 24

Kung Fu Diagram...................... 22
Glossary 30
Read More 31
Internet Sites........................ 31
Index................................ 32

CHAPTER 1
THE SHAOLIN TEMPLE

Mystery surrounds the history of kung fu. Some people think kung fu began hundreds of years ago. Chinese **monks** may have started the martial art. The monks lived in the Shaolin Temple in eastern China.

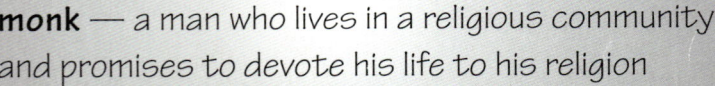

monk — a man who lives in a religious community and promises to devote his life to his religion

the bell tower of the Shaolin Temple

Thieves stole treasure from the temple hundreds of years ago. The monks did not know how to fight. They could not protect the temple.

Monks still live in the Shaolin temple today.

Some people then believe a monk named Bodhidharma visited the temple. He taught the monks kung fu. Today, there are many styles of kung fu. Most people practice **Shaolin kung fu.**

MARTIAL ARTS FACT

Other styles of kung fu include Tai Chi, Wing Chun, and Choy Lay Fut.

Shaolin kung fu — the most popular style of kung fu; people believe the style began at the Shaolin Temple.

children practicing kung fu in China

CHAPTER 2
PRACTICING KUNG FU

Kung fu fighters wear special pants and a jacket. Their uniforms can be black, red, or white.

Kung fu fighters learn new moves from a **sifu**. A sifu teaches fighters how to kick and strike. They also learn how to grapple and trap. Fighters trap opponents by holding their arms and using strikes.

sifu — the Chinese word for teacher

13

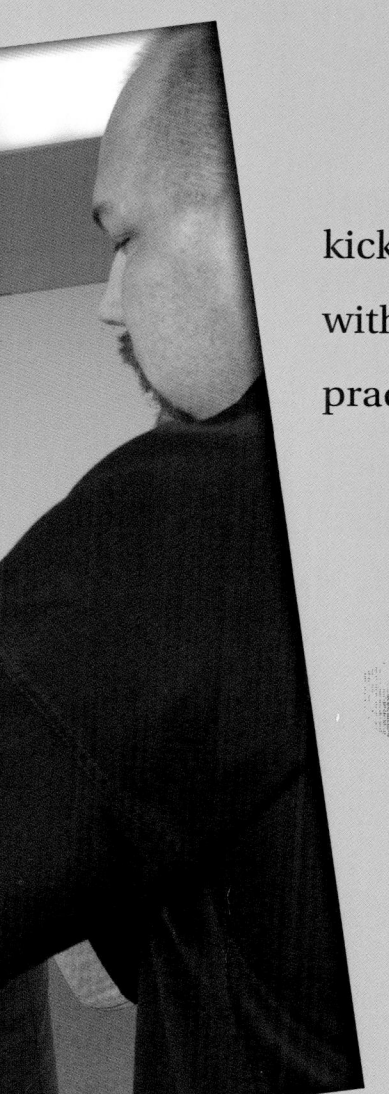

Fighters practice their punches and kicks on bags. These bags can be filled with sand, rice, or beans. Fighters also practice hitting a **dummy**.

MARTIAL ARTS FACT

Kung fu fighters may also practice with swords or staffs.

dummy — a wooden or plastic figure made to look like a human body

Kung fu fighters learn to move like animals. In the tiger style, fighters pretend their hands are claws. The fighters pounce like tigers. Other styles include snake, crane, and praying mantis.

tiger style

CHAPTER 3
COLORS AND RANKS

Kung fu fighters wear colored belts or **sashes** to show their ranks. Many beginners wear a white sash.

MARTIAL ARTS FACT

Not all kung fu schools use the same colors to show rank.

sash — a wide strip of cloth worn around the waist to show a kung fu fighter's rank

Fighters earn a different colored sash for each rank. Fighters must learn new kicks and strikes to earn a different sash. It takes at least three years to reach the highest rank.

MARTIAL ARTS FACT

Sash colors include white, yellow, and blue. Sashes can also be green, red, or brown.

KUNG FU DIAGRAM

HIGH FRONT KICK

CHAPTER 4
KUNG FU COMPETITIONS

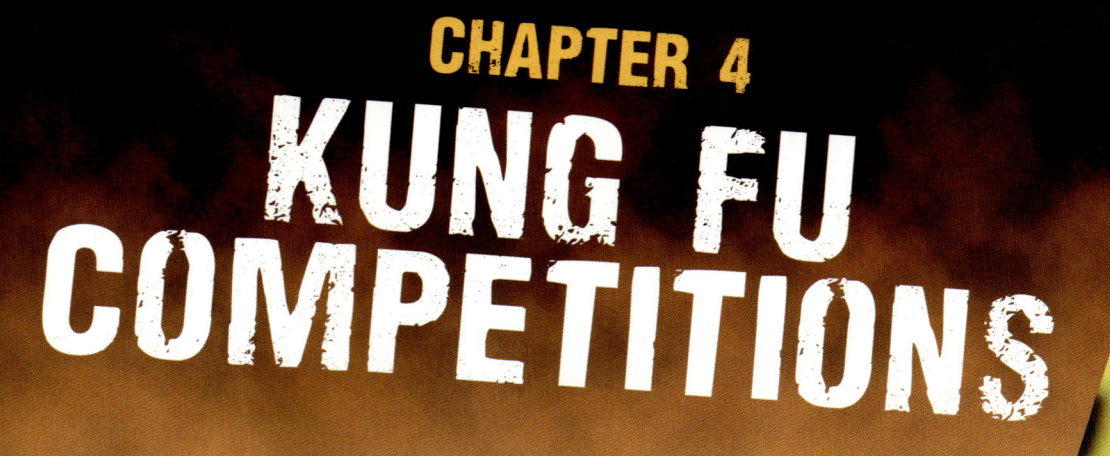

Fighters compete in tournaments. The World Wushu Championships are held every two years. The first-place fighter earns a gold medal. Second and third place fighters earn the silver and bronze medals.

MARTIAL ARTS FACT

Martial arts are called *wushu* in China.

Actor Bruce Lee made kung fu famous with movies like *Enter the Dragon*. Today, people see amazing kung fu moves from Jet Li and Jackie Chan. Movies are just another reason people love kung fu's high-action moves!

MARTIAL ARTS FACT

In movies, kung fu is called "wire fu." Wires, harnesses, and other special effects help actors do moves in midair.

GLOSSARY

dummy (DUM-me) — a wooden or plastic figure made to look like a human body

grapple (GRAP-uhl) — grabbing someone without punching or kicking

monk (MUHNGK) — a man who lives in a religious community and promises to devote his life to his religion

sash (SASH) — a wide strip of cloth worn around the waist to show a kung fu fighter's rank

Shaolin kung fu (SHOU-lin KUHNG FOO) — the most popular style of kung fu; people believe the style began at the Shaolin Temple.

sifu (SEE-foo) — the Chinese word for teacher

staff (STAF) — a stick or pole used as a weapon

style (STILE) — the way in which something is done

READ MORE

Eng, Paul. *Kungfu For Kids.* Tuttle Martial Arts for Kids. Boston: Tuttle, 2005.

Figueroa, Jose, and Stephan Berwick. *Tai Chi for Kids.* Boston: Tuttle, 2006.

Heinrichs, Ann. *Kung Fu and Tai Chi.* Kids' Guides to Martial Arts. Chanhassen, Minn.: Child's World, 2004.

INTERNET SITES

FactHound offers a safe, fun way to find Internet sites related to this book. All of the sites on FactHound have been researched by our staff.

Here's how:
1. Visit www.facthound.com
2. Choose your grade level.
3. Type in this book ID **1429619635** for age-appropriate sites. You may also browse subjects by clicking on letters, or by clicking on pictures and words.
4. Click on the **Fetch It** button.

FactHound will fetch the best sites for you!

INDEX

belts. *See* sashes
Bodhidharma, 8

Chan, Jackie, 26
competitions, 24

dummies, 15

Enter the Dragon, 26

Lee, Bruce, 26
Li, Jet, 26

medals, 24
monks, 4, 6, 8
moves
    grappling, 13
    kicks, 13, 15, 20, 26
    punches, 15
    strikes, 13, 20
    trapping, 13

sashes, 18, 20
Shaolin kung fu, 8
Shaolin Temple, 4, 6, 8
sifu, 13
styles
    Choy Lay Fut, 8
    crane, 16
    praying mantis, 16
    snake, 16
    Tai Chi, 8
    tiger, 16
    Wing Chun, 8

uniforms, 10

weapons, 15
wire fu, 26
World Wushu
    Championships, 24